LUNAR INTENTIONS

A YEARLONG JOURNAL FOR
NEW MOON INTENTION SETTING

SARA MCCORMICK

Content

INTRODUCTION

The Moon. La Luna. She shines down on us and illuminates the night sky, filling our hearts with wonder. We look for her in vain when she is New. And we celebrate her guiding light when she is Full. We track her, we follow her, and we are fascinated by her mysterious beauty.

For eons, the Moon has enchanted the human race. As a result, we have created myths surrounding the Moon and why she is chased across the night sky, just to hide and then reappear. We learned her phases and started tuning into her rhythms, using her light to our advantage. This light guided us when we needed to see our way home or be able to hunt in the darkness. We used the Moon phases to mark the passage of time and the best times for fishing, planting, and harvesting. Even today, some track the passage of time with a lunar calendar rather than a solar calendar.

Because of this connection with the Moon, it is no surprise that we would find a link on a spiritual or magical level. When we connect this way with the Moon's rhythms, we open up to her magic and energy. Then, using that energy, we find that we can use the Moon phases to draw what we desire closer to us and release what is holding us back.

As we learned and discovered more about the Moon over time, we started charting and tracking the Moon phases. We discovered that each Moon cycle, from New Moon to New Moon, is about 30 days. There are 8 lunar phases during that month, and each phase lasts a few days.

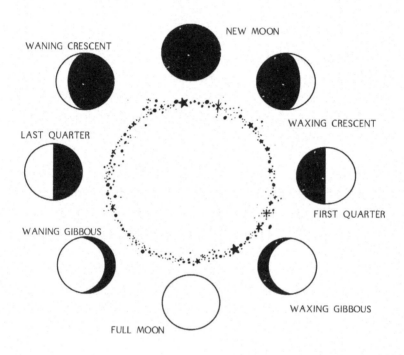

Now even though there are technically eight Moon phases, years of practice have taught me that it's easier to just work with the main four. In the past when I've tried to work with all eight Moon phases, I felt scattered and chaotic, that things were moving too quickly for me to get a handle on. Scaling back to just four phases gave me the room I needed to truly drop into my intentions for each phase, without feeling rushed or stretched too thin. Everything flowed with ease, and I felt more grounded overall.

SIMPLIFYING THE MOON PHASES

The four Moon phases I use are the New Moon, First Quarter Moon, Full Moon, and Last Quarter Moon.

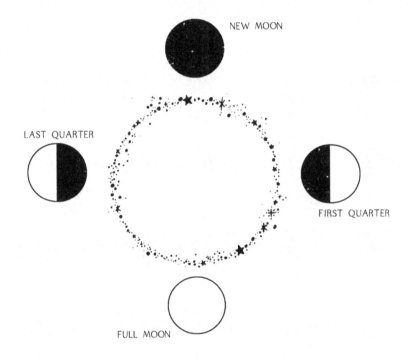

Utilizing these main four phases into my practice means I have a little more time with each phase, and don't feel pressed or hectic like I did trying to work with all eight phases. Each phase astronomically occurs as a specific time, but the energy can be felt for up to three days before and three days after the exact phase happens, meaning there is about a week to tap into the energy.

The four Moon phases together follow a pattern or a cycle. It goes New Moon to First Quarter Moon to Full Moon to Last Quarter Moon and then starts again.

As the Moon changes phases, going from the New Moon to the Full Moon, the light of the Moon changes. The Moon is fully dark at the New Moon and completely illuminated at the Full Moon. The light is increasing during the Waxing Moon and decreasing during the Waning Moon.

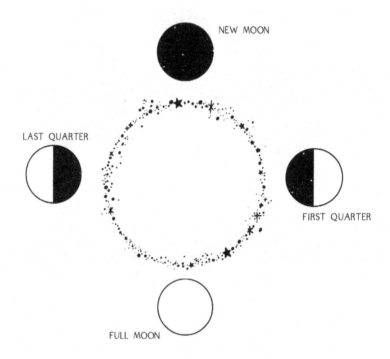

Most people will also say that they feel the lunar energies build and change as the Moon changes phase. We've all heard the comments about the light of a Full Moon changing human behavior! The New Moon a time of inward reflection, where the Full Moon is for outward expression.

Typically with any spiritual or metaphysical work, the
Waxing Moon (light increasing) is a time for attracting or calling
in energies, and the Waning Moon (light decreasing) is a time for
releasing and banishing. The New Moon is a time for intention
setting for the lunar month ahead, and the Full Moon is where you
celebrate and the results of your work.

Another way to look at the four Moon phases is akin to the seasons of the year.

New Moon: Winter, a time of rest and dreaming of the year ahead.

First Quarter Moon: Spring, when we plant seeds and begin the
work.

Full Moon: Summer, everything is in full growth and bloom.

Last Quarter Moon: Fall, harvest, and thanks for the bounty.

Many apps and calendars show the Moon phases if you're unsure
which phase we're in right now.

How to check the current moon phase
There are phone apps that will tell you the current moon phase,
such as Deluxe Moon.
Websites such as farmersalmanac.com and moonconnection.com
can also be used to check in on the current Moon phase.

WHY USING THE MOON PHASES WORKS

Now that you understand what the moon phases are, you may be wondering why you should pay attention to the lunar cycle at all. How can the moon help you in creating the life you most desire?

I firmly believe the moon (as well as the stars, planets, and all the other parts of astrology) hold a certain magic. But most of that magic you. Using the lunar cycle as a framework for taking action towards the dreams we want to manifest, we are tapping into our magic that we hold as beings of this Universe. This magic is your emotions! Our feelings directly impact our bodies at a cellular level and correlate to changes in our magnetic field. This correlation is why getting in touch with your emotions is the number one key for both manifestation and living a life in flow and harmony.

During the New Moon phase, you create sacred space, tap into the depths of your feelings around your dreams, shift your emotional body into alignment with your goals, and give yourself time to get in touch with what you want. All of that is magic.

With the First Quarter Moon, you start taking action. You do research and make a plan. You talk with others and get them involved. You get things moving, which is magic all of its own that sends ripples out into the Universe. Taking action while having clarity on the feelings behind your intention is like using a magnet to draw what you want closer to you.

As the Full Moon rolls around, you shift your mindset to gratitude and celebration, pausing to recognizing your hard work and feeling proud of what you have accomplished. We know from science that gratitude and self-recognition of our accomplishments help rewire our minds, so we are more resilient, hopeful, and optimistic. Again, all helping put you in that emotional alignment we're seeking for manifestation.

And finally, with the Last Quarter Moon, we turn to rest and retreat. Letting go of whatever didn't work out for us and mindfully, making space for the new we know is just around the corner with the next lunar cycle. Rest is such an essential part of the lunar cycle and is a missing key in the day-to-day life of many of us. But, unfortunately, we never give ourselves the permission we seek to rest and end up burning out over and over again.

Which is another reason using the moon phases works.

It's a cycle of dream, action, celebration, and rest, a cycle our hustle culture pushes aside in favor of damaging productivity. Using the moon phases over time helps you find yourself again by centering two things:

1) Your feelings

and

2) Your natural cycles of rest and action

NEW MOON

The New Moon occurs is when the Moon is not visible in the sky because the Moon is directly between the Earth and the Sun. It is a time of new beginnings, like a seed being planted in the earth. It is a potent time for manifestation and dreaming of that which you want to create. Seasonally, it is Winter when everything is gathering energy underground in preparation for Springtime.

The New Moon is time for intention setting and dreaming, but not action, not just yet. You want to simmer in the potential for a little while, like a seed opening up underground and sending roots into the soil for water and nourishment. Focus on your roots before your sprout upward.

But just because you shouldn't act doesn't mean you can't plan. This dreaming time can be helpful for researching and planning for the First Quarter Moon phase when it will be time to take action towards your intention.

Feel free to do a lot of dreaming and catnapping during the New Moon time, using vision boards to make your goals and intentions more concrete. The aim here is to dream big and not limit yourself but feel into your intention not only the day of the New Moon but every day after as well.

When we set an intention at the New Moon, the energy carries forward for months, sometimes years if we're working with an eclipse, but our time working with that intention is done at the Full Moon. So that is why it is important to spend with your intention after the New Moon and take action steps towards it around the First Quarter Moon. Because at the Full Moon we take time to celebrate all our hard work and efforts.

Don't be afraid of this step! When we get an idea, we often want to rush ahead right to taking action and getting the ball rolling, but first, we need to take time to get super clear on our feelings behind that idea. We'll dive more into that when we start talking about exactly how we set our New Moon intentions in the next chapter.

New Moon Correspondences

Tarot: The Fool

Herbs: Mugwort, primrose, vervain, wormwood

Animals: Hawk, leopard, magpie, tiger

Color: Black, silver

Gemstones: Black moonstone, iolite, labradorite

Moon rise: The New Moon rises very close with the Sun, so it's too close to be seen.

NEW MOON RITUALS

The New Moon is the time to set an intention or goal for the upcoming lunar cycle. It's a time to begin something new or start a new cycle, so it's essential to get crystal clear on your goal and, more importantly, the feelings you have behind it.

Connecting with the feelings behind your intention is the key to manifesting your heart's desires and bringing your intention to fulfillment.

Some rituals ideas:
Write down your intention - it can even be a list! Then, put it somewhere you will see it often.

Meditate while holding a piece of labradorite.

Journal as if you had already manifested your intention. What does that look like?

Research on a plan and create action steps to take during the First Quarter Moon.

magic

DREAM MAP RITUAL

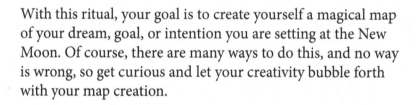

Materials
A large piece of paper
Several small candles
Something to draw with - pencils, markers, paint, whatever
strikes your fancy!

With this ritual, your goal is to create yourself a magical map
of your dream, goal, or intention you are setting at the New
Moon. Of course, there are many ways to do this, and no way
is wrong, so get curious and let your creativity bubble forth
with your map creation.

At one end of your paper, write down your goal. Check out
the chapter on intention setting for more details here. Still,
you'll want to make sure that you word your intention in the
present tense (such as I am peaceful) and that is it as clear
and specific as possible (for example, if your intention is
around a money goal, name exactly what that goal is down to
the last penny).

On the opposite end of your paper, draw you! You can be
elaborate here with a drawing of you, use a photograph of
you that you glue to tape to the paper, or simply write 'me.'
Follow your instincts here!

Now comes the fun part! First, you'll want to list out all the steps of how you'll get from where you are to where you want to go. Then, you can simply write them out, draw them, paste images onto your paper with tape or stickers. These steps make up the road on the map from you to your dream. They're the guideposts that will help you find your way.

Get as creative as you want here. Perhaps your road is straight across your paper, or maybe it curves and loops along with the page. Either way is perfect.

Now take your small candles, and place them on the paper next to each step on the road, marking the guideposts that will guide you over the coming weeks. Light each candle one by one and imagine yourself as you complete each step. What do you look like as you complete the steps? Who is helping you? Where are you located? And most importantly, how do you feel?

If you're able, let the candles burn while you sit in the energy of the dream you're conjuring and calling to you.

You are absolute magic.

NEW MOON JOURNAL PROMPTS

Journaling with the moon phases is a great way to slow down and tune in with their energy, as well as receive insight from your intuition. Try working with the journal questions below during the New Moon for additional guidance.

-What do you want to call into your life?

-What do you want more of in your life?

-How do you feel at this New Moon?

-What in your life needs a fresh start?

-What seeds do you want to plant in your life right now?

New Moon Card Spread

Use your favorite tarot or oracle card for additional insight into what the New Moon may be bringing up for you.

1. Your Current State

2. What do you wish to grow?

3. How can you fertilize and tend to the seeds you are planting?

4. How can you lean into trust during this lunar cycle?

5. How can you express yourself more fully?

FIRST QUARTER MOON

The First Quarter Moon is when the right half of the Moon is illuminated, and the left half is dark (in the Southern Hemisphere it is the opposite, with the left side illuminated and the right side dark). Energy is starting to build at this time, and you should use that energy for action! The plans you made during the New Moon are now getting implemented, and actionable items are put on the calendar.

The First Quarter Moon is similar to a seed that has begun to grow and is flourishing but not blooming.

This time is when you should take action regarding your New Moon intention and get the ball rolling. Open that store, release that product, go to that new class, put that dating profile online!

A crucial part of keeping the energy up during this time is to spend time with your intention each day. Have faith that your consistent efforts in moving forward and keeping your momentum up will pay off.

You can also look at this First Quarter Moon as being like Spring when you have planted seeds and begin the work of tending to them.

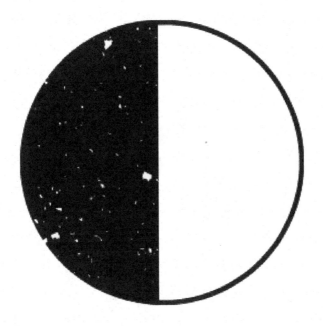

You are outside working, pruning the plants, and fertilized your tender seedlings. This is where the daily tending and action comes in of the intentions we set at the New Moon. We don't just plant the seeds and walk away, assuming the plant will grow. We water it daily, we fertilize it, we make sure it is getting enough sunlight and nutrients. We must tend to our New Moon intentions in the same way, taking actions that support our intention and displaying that we are willing to do the work. For example, if your intention was to create habits that support your health, what actions could you take around that intention? Perhaps you get a large water bottle to carry around with you all day to increase your water intake. Or maybe you spend one evening a week meal planning and grocery shopping for the week ahead, so you have healthy food options available to you.

First Quarter Moon Correspondences

Tarot: The Magician

Herbs: Cinnamon, gardenia, peppermint

Animals: Beaver, horse, wolf

Color: Green, orange, yellow

Gemstones: Carnelian, ocean jasper, lapis lazuli, sunstone

Moon rise: The First Quarter Moon rises around noon, and it sets around midnight.

FIRST QUARTER MOON RITUALS

Action steps are steps you take towards your New Moon intention. They are actions that show the Universe that you are willing and able to do the work to meet the Universe halfway. Setting an intention is just part of the work. You must sit with that intention and make strides towards it.

For example, if you set an Intention towards increasing your finances, do you have a budget? Are you sticking to it? Are you setting aside money in a savings account? Are you investing? Are you working on your money blocks and your relationship with money?

Some rituals ideas:
Launch a new project.

Begin a new daily habit or routine.

Plan out the steps you'll take over
the next week to move closer
to your intention.

STANDING IN YOUR POWER RITUAL

Materials
Journal
An object to act as a tailsman or a reminder of your power
Candle

For this ritual, you'll need a journal, talisman, and a candle. The candle can be any color because I believe it is the intention that genuinely matters! But if you have a candle that is the color that feels like power to you, by all means, use it. For some folks, this is deep red, and others gravitate towards a bright purple. Use what color resonates for you.

For your object, choose something that will be in a place you will easily see it each day, or pick something that you can wear each day, such as a favorite necklace or ring. Gemstones, painted rocks, statues, and even a picture of yourself are all great options.

To begin the ritual, you'll want to set your space with intention. You don't need to do or wear anything fancy here, but you do need to take a few moments to ground and center. Take a few deep breaths in and out, and let your mind let go of the chatter and worries of the day. Sometimes music playing softly in the background can help with this.

When you feel ready, light your candle and spend a few minutes writing in your journal and asking yourself the following questions.

-What does power mean to me?

-What does power feel like to me?

-Do I own my power or give it away?

-How can I reclaim my power?

After thinking about the themes, those questions brought up for you, grab your talisman and hold it in your hands. Close your eyes and visualize yourself claiming all of your power.

What does that person look like? What are they wearing? How do they speak and act? Envision all the parts of this person as you are able.

Gently shift your attention to your hands holding your talisman. Imagine the power, magic, and essence of the The person you saw in your mind transferring to the talisman, bolstering your courage, confidence, and faith in yourself each time you see or wear it.

FIRST QUARTER MOON JOURNAL PROMPTS

Journaling with the moon phases is a great way to slow down and tune in with their energy, as well as receive insight from your intuition. Try working with the journal questions below during the First Quarter Moon for additional guidance.

-What actions are you taking towards your New Moon intention?

-What obstacles or roadblocks are in your way?

-What area of your life needs some extra energy?

-Who can help hold you accountable as you strive towards your goal?

First Quarter Moon Card Spread

Use your favorite tarot or oracle card for additional insight into what the First Quarter Moon may be bringing up for you.

1. What area of your life needs attention so your New Moon intention can blossom?

2. What skills or talents can help you reach your goal?

3. Who in your life can support you in your dreams?

FULL MOON

The Full Moon is when the Moon is fully illuminated, as the Moon and Sun are on opposite ends of the Earth. It is a time of celebration and receiving. Take the time to acknowledge your accomplishments and harvest the fruits of your labors.

If you have something to share or celebrate, now is the time, even if you feel unsure or not ready. The Full Moon brings the spotlight, and this exposure can seem intimidating. However, as the energy and emotions build, the light can also reveal the hidden and unexpected. During the Full Moon, what has been manifesting since the New Moon is fully illuminated and will continue to grow over the next six months. Your New Moon intention you set this lunar cycle with culminate with the Full Moon of the same zodiac sign of the New Moon you set your intention in.

The building of this energy can seem overwhelming or hectic. But don't worry if you don't have all the answers just now. Do your best to ride the wave of energy, as it will lessen after the Full Moon, and the Waning Moon may bring solutions. If you struggle with the Full Moon with headaches or insomnia, grounding meditations may help.

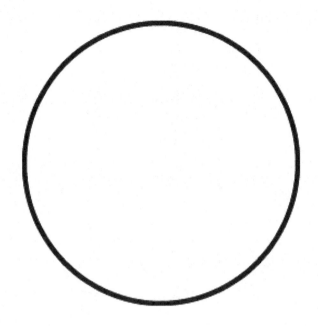

When we set an intention at the New Moon, the energy carries forward for months, sometimes years if we're working with an eclipse, but our time working with that intention is done at the Full Moon. So that is why it is so important to spend with your intention after the New Moon and take action steps towards it around the First Quarter Moon. Because at the Full Moon we take time to celebrate all our hard work and efforts.

Because of the emphasis on celebration and completion, a Full Moon is the perfect time for gratitude rituals, for connecting with others, and recognizing what is abundant and joyful in your life right now. A lot of us gloss over the act of celebrating our efforts and accomplishments and jump right back into toiling away at another task or project. Use this time to shift that focus and do something to celebrate yourself.

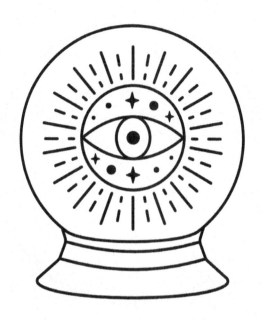

Full Moon Correspondences

Tarot: The Chariot

Herbs: Bergamot, honeysuckle, myrrh, sandalwood

Animals: Cow, lion, peacock

Color: Blue, green, gold, turquoise

Gemstones: Herkimer diamond, jade, moonstone, selenite

Moon rise: The Moon is opposite of the Sun. So it rises as the Sun sets, and sets as the Sun rises.

FULL MOON RITUALS

You may find that something comes to light around the time of a Full Moon or is illuminated for you. After all, Full Moons are radiant and brighten the night sky, and this moonlight can be reflected in your life by revealing a pathway you hadn't noticed before - it may even correspond to the intention you set as the previous New Moon.

Some rituals ideas:
Write down three things you are grateful for.

Do something to celebrate your hard work - have a dance party, eat a slice of cake, gaze at the moon.

Charge your crystals (simply put them where they will 'see' the light of the moon).

Take a bath.

Meditate.

FULL MOON BATH RITUAL

Materials
Clear quartz
Sea salt
Dried herbs or flowers

Full Moons bring about an intensity that you can't ignore, often arriving with a wave of emotion that you have to surrender to and ride the wave. A Full Moon bath ritual is a great way to do this!

Before you begin, you'll want to make sure your space is clean and feels welcoming and cozy. Perhaps you have a favorite towel or robe you'll wish to have nearby or some scented candles that always help you wind down.

If you have relaxing crystals or gemstones that correspond to the Full Moon (see page 34), you can place them around your tub. However, if you want to put any crystals in your tub, make sure they are water safe first, such as clear quartz.

As you run your bath, imagine the water is shimmering with a soft white glow, like your bathwater is infused with healing and magical moonlight.

Toss the sea salt and herbs into your bathwater. Go with the amount that feels right for you, but a good general rule of thumb is a quarter cup of sea salt for medicinal benefits, such as easing tired muscles or soothing itchy skin.

Below are some herbs that you may like to use:
-Lavender: For relaxation and peace.
-Rose: Anti-inflammatory, antibacterial, and it softens and tones the skin.
-Sage: Sage is antibacterial, and so it helps with skin inflammation, such as eczema or acne.
-Passionflower: Another calming herb that gently relaxes.
-Eucalyptus: Perfect for cold and flu season.
-Chamomile: Pairs beautifully with lavender for a nighttime relaxation bath.
-Marigold: Also known as Calendula. Perfect for soothing irritated skin.

As you soak in your bath, visualize the shimmering water clearing away any negativity. Trust that whatever the Full Moon is illuminating for you at this time is just one chapter in a bigger story that you do not yet know. And that's okay.

You don't need to have all the answers right now. You just need to be able to let go and ride the wave.

FULL MOON
JOURNAL PROMPTS

Journaling with the moon phases is a great way to slow down and tune in with their energy, as well as receive insight from your intuition. Try working with the journal questions below during the Full Moon for additional guidance.

-What has grown over the past two weeks?

-What themes or situations have repeatedly shown up for you lately?

-What feels rich and abundant right now?

-What feels like it is coming to a close or ending a cycle in your life?

Full Moon Card Spread

Use your favorite tarot or oracle card for additional insight into what the Full Moon may be bringing up for you.

1. Your Current State

2. What is being illuminated in your life right now?

3. What has manifested since the New Moon?

4. What needs to be celebrated and recognized?

5. What message does the Universe have for you?

LAST QUARTER MOON

The Last Quarter Moon is when the left half of the Moon is illuminated, and the right half is dark (opposite for the Southern Hemisphere). This is a time when you look at what seeds you sowed during the New Moon. Which seeds grew and which did not? Make notes and prepare to make any adjustments as needed for the next cycle. Then, release what you need to rest and begin the process again.

The Last Quarter Moon is also an excellent time to release whatever is stuck or stagnant. Whatever you need to wrap up and move on from, now is a good time to do so.

The release can be sad for some, as it can be difficult to release something you hoped would grow. But this release makes room for something new and perhaps better.

This time is also good to start to rest and store up our energy for the new lunar cycle ahead of us. Just as Nature needs time to sleep each year before the growing seasons, we humans need our rest as well, and the Waning Moon is here to remind of this need.

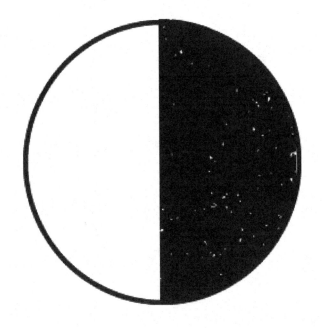

The Last Quarter Moon is similar to Autumn when we are giving thanks and recognizing our bounty and storing and preparing for the Winter ahead. It is when we can the remaining fruits and vegetables and remove any dead or abandoned growth. The fields are usually cleared and fertilized so they can recover nutrients for planting again next Spring. Many harvest festivals happen in the Fall, where we eat the food we grew and give thanks for the growing season's bounty. The same applies to the intention you set at the New Moon. Now is the time to give thanks for whatever growth or results you saw. This is also the time to release what did not grow, and make sure you are doing what you need to do to rest and recover, nourish yourself, so you have the energy to get back to work again at the First Quarter Moon / Spring. Perhaps during the Last Quarter Moon time, you like to get a massage, go to therapy, or simply do a lot of journaling. Whatever internal and external work you need to do to release and rest, now is the time for it.

Last Quarter Moon Correspondences

Tarot: Wheel of Fortune

Herbs: Cypress, lavender, patchouli, sage, st. john's wort

Animals: Bat, dolphin

Color: Dark blue, dark purple

Gemstones: Bronzite, rose quartz, sodalite, sugilite

Moon rise: During the Last Quarter Moon, the Moon rises around midnight and sets around noon.

LAST QUARTER MOON RITUALS

When the moon is waning, it decreases in light. As the moon darkens, now is the time to release whatever is stuck or stagnant. The release can be sad, as it can be difficult to remove something that you had hoped would grow or be different. But this release makes room for something new and perhaps better. Releasing during the Waning Moon is preparation for the New Moon, a time of new beginnings and fresh starts.

Some ritual ideas:
Write down what you are releasing and burn the paper.

Write down what you are releasing and bury the paper.

Write down what you are releasing and tear the paper up into smaller pieces and throw them away.

Take a bath or shower and imagine the water washing away anything energetically stuck to you or holding you back.

BURN IT AWAY RITUAL

Materials
Pen and paper
Fireproof vessel
Lighter or match

The Last Quarter Moon is a time of releasing and letting go, but this can often be hard to do without a visual for our minds to process, especially if you're working on releasing something intangible, such as a habit or negative thinking pattern.

As always, when mindfully working with magic, you'll want to set the stage. Clear your space and spend a few minutes grounding and centering yourself. Grounding for you may look like bringing your attention to your breath, doing a guided visualization, journaling to get your thoughts out of your head and onto paper, or listening to music and moving your body.

Next, write what you want to let go down on a piece of paper. Write it ALL down. Every feeling, every doubt, everything that sets your nerves alight with anger, or whatever it is that you need to release. Write it down.

Don't censor or judge yourself here. This piece of paper is a safe space to get out all the emotions and thoughts that are currently feeling stuck and stagnant in your body that you need to release and move on from.

If left to be ignored or glossed over, these feelings can morph and feel like chains dragging you down.

Once you're done writing, you'll want to get a fireproof vessel that you can use to burn the paper. Many stores sell cast iron mini cauldrons that work great for this purpose. It's also wise to be sure you're not near any smoke detectors, or perhaps go outside for this next step.

Light your list with a lighter or match, and place it in your fireproof vessel.

Watch and breathe as your paper burns, feeling your body relax as it releases the weight of what is burning.

LAST QUARTER MOON JOURNAL PROMPTS

Journaling with the moon phases is a great way to slow down and tune in with their energy, as well as receive insight from your intuition. Try working with the journal questions below during the Last Quarter Moon for additional guidance.

-How did this lunar cycle feel to you?

-What are you releasing right now?

-What did you learn over the past few weeks?

-What can you do to refill your cup between now and the next New Moon?

-What self-care does your soul need right now?

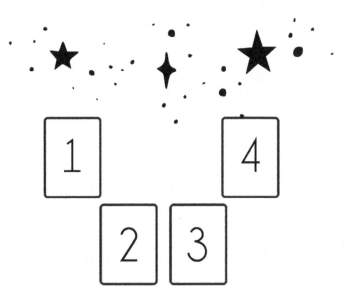

Last Quarter Moon Card Spread

Use your favorite tarot or oracle card for additional insight into what the Last Quarter Moon may be bringing up for you.

1. What is no longer serving me?

2. How can I release what is holding me back?

3. Who or what can support me in letting go?

4. How can I nourish myself and refill my cup?

SETTING AN INTENTION

The New Moon is perfect for manifestation magic, and therefore just the right time to set an intention for the upcoming lunar month, as well as the next six months ahead. What is an intention? An intention is a specific goal or desire you have, something you're striving for or looking to manifest in your life. But what makes an intention unique is the way you look at it. These New Moon intentions tend to work best when they are feeling based and specific.

Being able to feel your intention with all of your senses is the key to manifestation.

See what it looks like in your mind's eye, and incorporate any textures, smells, specific colors, or sounds with it. The more specific you can get, the better. For example, it's not just a car you want; it's a 1972 Corvette Convertible in Sunfire Yellow with a black leather interior, white line tires, turbo hydra-matic automatic transmission, and AM/FM radio stereo. You can smell the leather and feel the rumble of the engine. In your mind, you can see how that Sunfire Yellow will look sitting next to your blue house. And, of course, how you feel when driving your car lights you up with so much joy that you're practically vibrating. Now we're talking magic.

The difference between goals and intentions

One may think that intentions are the same thing as goals, but there are slight differences between the two. Remember, intentions are specific, but they are feeling-based. Goals can be precise, but they are usually number-based.

Let's break this down with something that many folks start with when beginning intention setting: gaining money.

They'll set an intention such as 'I want to make money this month.' Some folks may go further and get specific by saying, 'I want to make $10,000 this month'. But that is a goal and not an intention. There are no feelings involved.

An intention for that could be 'I feel grounded and secure. I am receiving a steady flow of financial abundance this month'.

Let's work through another one. A beginner might make an intention of 'I want to lose weight". But that's not quite an intention yet.

So how do we turn this goal into an intention? Thinking about what it would feel like to lose weight. How would your body feel? Your mind? What steps would you need to take to support that intention? Your new intention might be 'I feel my body in its perfect state as I intuitively nurture and strengthen it.'

this

Doesn't that new intention just light you up and fill you with warmth and gladness? A good intention should!

Now, goals are great to go along with intentions, but in my experience, I've been pleasantly surprised when I made the intention more about the action feeling (releasing, deepening, feeling, awakening, attracting, connecting...) than the goal (gain $10,000, lose 20 lbs, sell X number of things).

A note on intention wording
An important thing to remember when going about your intention setting is that the New Moon is the time when the Moon is growing in light. Because of that, you'll want your New Moon intentions ideally to be about abundance: attracting, building, developing, nurturing. If your intention is to release something, you'll want to re-focus that releasing onto the positive feelings you'll have once that thing is removed. Or you'll want to save that intention for the Full Moon, or just after when the Moon is waning – the time of releasing.

That's why in the weight loss example above, the intention wasn't about the act of losing weight. It was about the feelings felt after the weight loss had already occurred. It was about the feelings of peace, joy, strength, and confidence that increased due to the weight decreasing.

Just remember, the Waxing Moon is for growing, attracting, and increasing, while the Waning Moon is for decreasing, releasing, and letting go.

That leads to the next point. You should state intentions in the present tense. Don't say 'if' or 'when' or 'I will'. Instead, say 'I am'.

Your intentions should be worded as if they are already happening. Seeing your intention in your mind's eye and speaking it out loud as if it has already happened is very powerful. It is a signal to the Universe. You're saying, 'I'm here, and I'm ready.'

Picking your intention

Sometimes it may be hard or intimidating to pick an intention. There seem to be limitless options, and it can be overwhelming to narrow them down.

Some advice for settling on an intention is to ask for whatever resonates most fully with your body. Sit quietly and say out loud all the intentions you're thinking about working with. After you say each intention, take a few deep breaths and see how you feel. Does that intention weigh you down or lighten your spirits? Do you feel excited, alive, vibrating with that intention? Does it feel heavy like a burden? Pay attention to those feelings, and the one that resonates the most, the one that you can feel in your body, vibrating in your cells with possibility, that's the one you should focus on. It may be 'big' or 'small' – it doesn't matter!

What matters is how you feel about your intention - that's where all the power is.

INTENTION PRACTICE

Use these pages to practice writing intentions!
Remember: positive feelings & present tense.

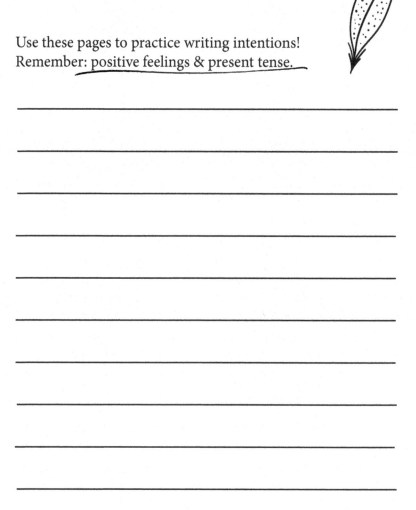

_____

_____

_____

_____

_____

_____

_____

_____

_____

Coming back to your intention each day

Outside of feeling your intention, the second most crucial thing for intention setting is coming back to it each day. If you can come back to that intention day after day in meditation and feel that intention, see it in your mind's eye and be excited about it each day, you're golden. That's why the feeling aspect of the worded intention is so important. It's a grounding rod to instantly get you back to that feeling state surrounding your intention. It helps you infuse your body with those feelings and drop in. Just five minutes a day of dropping into how your intention feels, imagining every aspect of it in your mind, and saying your intention out loud will lead to profound work on your part.

Final thoughts on intentions

And as always, when talking about New Moon intentions, one final note is that words are not enough. So even if you imagine your intention beautifully and craft the wording so that it lights you up every time you say it, that's not quite going far enough.

What are you doing to help your intention along? What work are you putting in? The Universe will only respond in kind. So if you're setting an intention without any work and wondering why your results aren't quite what you thought they'd be, take a look in the mirror.

That leads to the next point. When you word intentions, Using the examples from above if you're looking for more financial abundance…. do you have a budget? Do you stick to it? Do you overspend, or do you honor your flow of money? Is there something you should be doing/making/working on to create an avenue for money to flow?

key!

If you're looking to lose weight, how's your diet? Do you exercise? How is your self-care? Do you treat your body with respect?

There's always something you can do to help the Universe along and let it know that you're in this and willing to show up and do the work.

facts

Tools to help assist your intention setting
-Meditate on your intention. ~~See it in your mind's eye using~~ ~~Meditate on your intention.~~ First, see it in your mind's eye using all your senses. Then, feel free to hold any gemstones you feel called to that may correspond with your intention.

-Write your intention down somewhere you can see it every day and be reminded of it (and take any action necessary to help your intention along)

yes

-Make a vision board for your intention. Draw, paint, print out photos or cut photos or words up from magazines. Get creative!

yes

WHAT INTENTION SETTING MAY LOOK LIKE

Let's take a look at a couple of examples of New Moon intention setting.

Julie
The day of the New Moon has arrived, and Julie couldn't be more excited. She had previously marked the day and time in her calendar and made sure she had gathered all the tools she would need.

Julie sits in her garden in front of a large tree stump, which she uses as an altar. The scents of rose and jasmine float around her. Fireflies dance in the air, making the summer evening sky twinkle.

Julie takes comfort in working outside, with the elements, and her altar reflects that. In front of her, on the tree stump, sits a dried smudge stick of sage and mugwort, along with a candle, a glass of water, a bowl, her New Moon intention written on a piece of paper, and flowers Julie just picked from her garden.

She picks up a smudge stick and moves it around her space. She allows her breath to slow and deepen. Julie then lights her candle, pours the water from the cup into the bowl, and then places the flowers into the bowl. This ritual is one she has crafted and honed over the years to help her mind and body ground and center for any rituals she practices.

Julie brings her mind to the intention she had written earlier that day on the piece of paper before her. The New Moon is in Virgo, and Julie's attention aligns perfectly with it. She wants to bring her focus and attention to detail back to caring for her body in a nourishing, healthy way.

She pictures intention in her mind's eye and allows her body to feel her intention fuly. She can't help the smile that slowly spreads across her face as her body vibrates with joy.

Julie simply allows herself to see her intention as if it has already happened and fully experiences all the ways her intention will impact her life, taking as much time as she needs to fully drop into this New Moon intention.

She opens her eyes and brings her attention back to her breath. Then, picking up the piece of paper with her intention written on it, Julie carefully burns it with her candle before burying it in her garden, along with the flower and water mixture.

Julie stands and watches the sunset, giving thanks to the Universe before gently patting the earth where she just planted her New Moon intention.

Brianna

It's a crisp Autumn night, and Brianna is ready for the New Moon in Scorpio. She sits in the corner of her bedroom, full of soft pillows surrounding a small table. A sizeable star-shaped lantern hangs from the ceiling and casts a soft glow throughout the room while nearby speakers play music perfect for meditation.

On top of Brianna's altar sits a Ganesha statue with a jade and amethyst mala, along with some lit candles, gemstones, and her favorite tarot deck.

Brianna begins her ritual with a short grounding meditation. She has an idea for her New Moon intention, but she isn't 100% sure yet, so once she feels grounded, she turns her meditation into one of guidance, holding her favorite labradorite stone and clearing her mind for any insight that comes her way. Then, to clear her mind even further, after a few minutes, Brianna turns her attention to the Enya and Deva Premal coming from the speakers and lets her body intuitively move to the music.

While moving, Brianna is struck with inspiration and grabs her nearby journal, jotting down the thoughts and images that came to her regarding her New Moon intention. She now feels sure of her Intention and spends a great deal of time writing in her journal about it, taking care to explore all of her thoughts and letting her body feel all the feelings that come up around it.

With her intention in her mind, Brianna shuffles her tarot deck and pulls a few cards for guidance. She notes the cards and her interpretations of them in her journal before saying a prayer of gratitude and ending her ritual.

Make it your own

There are an endless amount of items you might use to craft your New Moon intention-setting ritual. Below you'll find a small list of tools you might find helpful when creating your sacred New Moon time.

-Bells
-Feathers
-Candles
-Incense
-Symbols of the four elements
-Tarot or Oracle cards
-Pendulums
-Statues of deities or animal guides
-Gemstones
-Smudge sticks
-Malas

Be sure to make yourself comfortable! Fill your space with soft pillows, warm blankets, soothing music, and twinkling lights - whatever you feel called to. Be sure to wear comfortable clothing, but a bonus if it's attire you feel empowered in and most like yourself.

After the New Moon

Working with your New Moon intention continues long after the New Moon occurs.

In the previous example, Julie's intention centered around caring for her body in a nourishing way. However, as the Moon started waxing and the First Quarter Moon rolled around, Julie might find that spending her Sunday morning going to the farmers market and meal prepping for the week ahead was what she needed to help ground her. This task helped her make better choices throughout the week, including moving her body more and sitting on the couch watching TV less.

With the Full Moon, Julie's new habits were starting to take root, and Julie celebrated having more energy. She made a gratitude list and looked forward to deepening her connection with her body over the upcoming months.

At the Last Quarter Moon, and throughout the following week where the Moon waned, Julie set aside some time to release her old fast food habit and examined what was no longer serving her and what she was ready to let go of.

As you can see, the work with your New Moon intention is ever-evolving and changes along with the Moon. This flow allows you to see and address your intention from every aspect. Using the phases this way also helps you tune into a wonderfully soothing rhythm of intention setting, action, celebration/gratitude, and release.

As humans, we can get caught up in the go-go-go mentality of always needing to be doing something more (and often, we tell ourselves, better).

The Moon herself is a beautiful reminder of balance and of giving ourselves time to shine, as well as rest. Just like the Moon waxes and wanes, changing from lightness to darkness, so should we be mindful of our times of action and relaxation.

RITUAL BRAINSTORMING

Let's brainstorm! Jot down all your ideas and inspiration for your New Moon rituals.

_____

_____

_____

_____

_____

_____

_____

_____

_____

MOON IN
THE SIGNS

As the Moon goes through all of the phases, she is also moving through zodiac signs. As a result, the Moon feels a little different in each sign, and the various signs favor different activities.

Knowing a little about how the Moon feels in each zodiac sign can be helpful for planning out your day, as well as thinking of an intention if you're stuck and unsure.

For example, on any day with the Moon in Aries, you may know that to watch out for tempers rising and not take any anger personally, as everyone is feeling it. But for a New Moon in Aries, you also know that any action taken during an Aries New Moon may not have sticking power, as Aries tends to get shiny object syndrome. So you choose to work on implementing a plan for a future project that month, since Aries is also a planning loving sign.

The following pages feature some quick and easy to understand guides of what the day might bring for you with the Moon in each sign, which can be helpful to integrate into your intention setting.

Aquarius

This Moon is all about connections and teamwork. Meetings, group activities, and connecting with old friends are all in order. You may find that you're a little more intuitive. Innovative Aquarius wants to improve things for the collective. Aquarius loves ideas but can find them hard to execute.

Pisces

Sensitive Pisces Moon usually means you'll be feeling all the feelings and creative expression is always an excellent way to process them. However, you may be more tired and intuitive than typical, so be sure to rest and hide away. Dreams can also be heightened.

Aries

Aries is the warrior sign. It acts (and reacts!) before thinking and is all about the self and individuality. A lack of patience and a high drive tend to give way to lots of action. You'll want to get moving to burn off some of that extra energy, or else you may find your temper has more of a bite than usual. Aries loves to plan, but actions taken during this Moon may lack staying power.

Taurus

Taurus is the sign that creates beauty. Taurus likes to take their time and experience all the sensual pleasures in life. So take care to enjoy the beauty around you and indulge in the small comforts, like flowers or a massage. Things started during a Taurus Moon have staying power. Taurus is also one of the two signs that deal with finances.

Gemini

The Gemini Moon is a Chatty Cathy. Got emails to catch up on? This talkative Moon is perfect for that. There is usually a bit of restless energy that is good for multitasking. Just be aware of this energy, so you don't burn out. The social Moon is an excellent time to catch up with friends or siblings, have a meeting, or go to a party.

Cancer

Moon in Cancer is very tenderhearted and sensitive, which may bring out our defenses prematurely. You may feel the extra need to eat comfort foods, as well as comfort others. Take time to reflect and acknowledge your emotions. This family-oriented Moon is all about your home and what makes you feel secure.

Leo

Shine on Leo Moon, shine on. This Moon is all about the expressive flair that one would expect from a lion. Energy may be spontaneous and incredibly passionate. Watch out for that stubborn streak, though! The Leo Moon wants to get things done.

Virgo

Get your clean on! The Moon in Virgo is a great time to do a deep cleaning of your home, organize your bills or sit down and make some to-do lists. This Moon may also mean you have a more difficult time hearing criticism. Virgo also rules all things health and fitness, especially holistic.

Libra

The Libra Moon tends to be very friendly and pleasant and likes to bring people together. Libra is all about balance, so be sure to look out for what is out of balance in your life. Look for the beauty around you and enjoy it, maybe even enhance it, as Libra loves close, intimate settings.

Scorpio

Time to get a little dark. The Scorpio Moon brings some weighty (and sometimes cynical) introspection with it. Your shadow self may want to come out and play. Let it. Scorpio rules all things dealing with sexuality, power, and letting go. Scorpio is the second sign that deals with money, specifically other people's money (think business deals).

Sagittarius

Are you ready for some adventure? The restless Sagittarius Moon is all about travel and exploration. Bringing some spontaneous energy, be prepared for plans to change. Just go with it! This Moon also loves learning and teaching. Sagittarius is one of the most spiritual of the signs, so connect with your higher power however you see fit.

Capricorn

Slow and steady wins the race when the Moon is in Capricorn. That goal may seem far away and out of reach, but just know one step at a time will get you there. Let this Moon's energy help you persevere and get down to business. This Moon is all about career, public image, and long-term goals.

DEEPER INTO THE SIGNS

Each zodiac sign identifies with an element, a quality, and is ruled by an astrological house. The elements, qualities, and houses are layers that you can use to dive deeper into the sign's meaning.

The Elements
All 12 astrological signs are divided into four main elements: earth, air, fire, and water.

Earth: Structure and form. They are making things happen. These signs are dependable and reliable and will see projects through. The Earth signs are Taurus, Virgo, and Capricorn.

Air: Communication and ideas. Restless, social, and spending a lot of time 'in the mind'. The Air signs are Gemini, Libra, and Aquarius.

Fire: Creativity and power. These signs have lots of energy and strong egos. Good at starting projects. The Fire signs are Aries, Leo, and Sagittarius.

Water: Emotional and sensitive. These signs feel very deeply and have strong family ties. The Water signs are Cancer, Scorpio, and Pisces.

The Qualities
The signs are also divided into three qualities: cardinal, fixed, and mutable.

Cardinal: Initiate and lead. Like to be in charge. The Cardinal signs are Aries, Cancer, Libra, and Capricorn.

Fixed: Builders and workhorses. Resistant to change. The Fixed signs are Taurus, Leo, Scorpio, and Aquarius.

Mutable: Travelers and like variety. Can adapt to new things. The Mutable signs are Gemini, Virgo, Sagittarius, and Pisces.

The qualities also relate to the seasons. The beginning of each season (Spring, Summer, Autumn, and Winter) is marked by the sun moving into a cardinal sign. The start of a new season brings in fresh energy and action, just like a cardinal sign.

The middle of the season is marked by the sun moving into a fixed sign, as the season is in full swing and is 'fixed'. You know which season you are in while you're in the middle of it!

And finally, the end of a season is ushered in by the sun moving into a mutable sign. This is when you can feel things changing in the air, even though you haven't shifted seasons yet.

DEEPER INTO
THE SIGNS

The Houses
Each sign is also ruled by one of the twelve houses.

1st House: Self-awareness, personal identity, appearance, beginnings, first impressions, approach to life. Ruled by Aries.

2nd House: Five senses, immediate environment, personal security, work, money, income, priorities, habits, self-worth. Ruled by Taurus.

3rd House: Communication, community, mental processes, learning style, siblings, hobbies. Ruled by Gemini.

4th House: Roots, emotional security, foundation, family, home, ancestry, self-care, women, nurturing, comfort in skin. Ruled by Cancer.

5th House: Self-expression, who you are, playfulness, creativity, fertility, romance, attraction, drama. Ruled by Leo.

6th House: Selfless service, health, fitness, medicine, organization, work habits, analytical thinking. Ruled by Virgo.

7th House: Companionship, relationship, partnership, marriage, business, contracts, interpersonal relationships. Ruled by Libra.

8th House: Sex, emotional intimacy, reproduction, shared assets, joint ventures and other people's resources, real estate, investments, spirituality, paranormal. Ruled by Scorpio.

9th House: Global knowledge, higher education, publishing, travel, law, religion, ethics, philosophy. Ruled by Sagittarius.

10th House: Career, ambition, worldly accomplishments, leadership, long term goals, father, masculinity, authority figures, boundaries. Ruled by Capricorn.

11th House: Humanitarianism, social awareness, friends, teamwork, utopian vision, technology, aviation/UFOs. Ruled by Aquarius.

12th House: Endings, closure, afterlife, the arts, holistic health, the unseen and unknown. Ruled by Pisces.

MOON IN ARIES

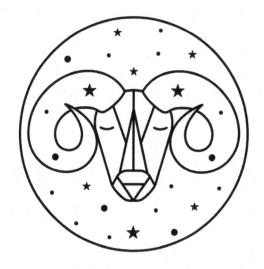

Aries Correspondences
House: 1st house

Element: Fire sign

Quality: Cardinal sign

Season: Spring

Planet: Mars

Colors: Pink, red, white, yellow

Chakras: Root, solar plexus, third eye

Body Parts: Head, face, eyes

Tarot: Emperor

Herbs: Basil, blackberry, cedar, carnation, dandelion, frankincense, garlic, juniper, peppermint, rosemary

Gemstones: Aventurine, bloodstone, carnelian, citrine, emerald, fire agate, garnet, ruby

Animals: Goat, magpie, ram, red-tailed hawk, woodpecker

Keywords
Acting first and thinking later, action, ambition, anger, assertiveness, business, courage, determination, energy, force, fresh starts, impatient, independence, jealousy, leadership, new beginnings, passion, selfish, wanting to go full speed, warrior energy

Shadow side
Laziness, impulsiveness

Things to do
Make a plan, make a decision, make a fresh start (Aries is the beginning of the zodiac, so it likes new starts), take a risk, work out, focus on self, pave a new trail, feelings come and go quickly, actions can lack staying power

Mantras
I believe in myself and my vision.
I have confidence in myself and my plan.
I am capable of making decisions and taking action.
I honor my passion.

MOON IN TAURUS

Taurus Correspondences
House: 2nd house

Element: Earth sign

Quality: Fixed sign

Season: Spring

Planet: Venus

Colors: Green, orange, light yellow, light blue

Chakras: Root, heart, throat

Body Parts: Throat, neck

Tarot: Hierophant

Herbs: Apple, blackberry, daisy, dandelion, cinquefoil, magnolia, hibiscus, lilac, mugwort, raspberry, sage

Gemstones: Carnelian, chrysocolla, emerald, iolite, malachite, moss agate, pyrite, topaz, tree agate, turquoise

Animals: Bull, dove, ox, robin, tiger

Keywords
Affection, beauty, connected to the body, endurance, grounding, indulgence, intuition, living it up, love, love of food, material things, money, order, passion, patience, pleasure, protection, security, sensuality, strength, vitality

Shadow side
Stubbornness, possessiveness

Things to do
Listen to your body, finish a project, stay at it, use your creative gift, garden, work on your self-worth, use a slow approach, appreciate beauty (go to a museum, eat good food, spend time in nature, get a massage), make a money plan, plant a garden

Mantras
Beauty can be fragile and strong.
I am leaning into trust.
I deserve a luxurious life.
I am creating financial independence in a joyful way.

MOON IN GEMINI

Gemini Correspondences
House: 3rd house

Element: Air sign

Quality: Mutable sign

Season: Spring

Planet: Mercury

Colors: Pink, violet, white, yellow, blue, green, orange

Chakras: Heart, throat

Body Parts: Shoulders, arms, hands, lungs

Tarot: The Lovers

Herbs: Bergamot, clover, lavender, lilac, hazel, mugwort, star anise, yarrow, walnut

Gemstones: Alexandrite, aquamarine, cat's eye, fluorite, howlite, moonstone, sapphire, tiger's eye

Animals: Deer, eagle, raven

Keywords
Adaptability, change, cleverness, communication, creativity, intelligence, open-mindedness, relationships, talking, the mind, truth, social butterfly. Gemini needs mental stimulation and creative outlets, represents the duality: within/without, feminine/masculine, shadow/light

Shadow Side
Switching emotions, playing tricks

Things to do
Read a new book, catch up with old friends, communicate, share information, write, meditate, look at things from a different perspective, share messages, write letters, tap into a creative outlet, Gemini can have a lot on the mind, so use mental stimulation and games to exercise the mind

Mantras
Words are abundantly flowing.
I am speaking with clarity.
I am honor my duality.

MOON IN CANCER

Cancer Correspondences
House: 4th house

Element: Water sign

Quality: Cardinal sign

Season: Summer

Planet: Moon

Colors: Light blue, gray, sea green, pink, yellow

Chakras: Sacral, solar plexus, heart

Body Parts: Chest, stomach, spine

Tarot: Chariot

Herbs: Agrimony, catnip, chamomile, gardenia, jasmine, lemon balm, marigold, violet

Gemstones: Amber, calcite, moonstone, opal, rose quartz, ruby, selenite, tiger's eye

Animals: Dog, blackbird, seagull, turtle

Keywords
Caregiving, creativity, dreams, emotions, empathic, family, femininity, home, introspection, intuition, love, Moon magic, mother, nature, nurturing, protection, romance, safety, sensitivity, sympathy, the metaphysical

Shadow side
Co-dependency, the shell aspect of cancer (think about a crab and the shell!) can seem cold or callous

Things to do
Re-organize home, repair home, anything to do with upgrading home or home safety, write, journal, review goals, take a nurturing bath, spend time with family, cook a nourishing meal, explore your family tree, watch a rom-com

Mantras
I honor my feelings.
I am safe.
I am radiating love and peace.

MOON IN LEO

Leo Correspondences
House: 5th house

Element: Fire sign

Quality: Fixed sign

Season: Summer

Planet: Sun

Colors: Green, gold, orange, red, yellow

Chakras: Solar plexus, heart

Body Parts: Heart, spine, upper back

Tarot: Strength

Herbs: Angelica, borage, cinnamon, goldenseal, heliotrope, honeysuckle, lavender, marigold, orange blossom, patchouli, rosemary, sunflower

Gemstones: Carnelian, citrine, danburite, garnet, herkimer diamond, jasper, labradorite, larimar, onyx, peridot, ruby, sunstone, tiger's eye

Animals: Doe, lion, eagle, peacock

Keywords
Action, ambition, arrogance, authority, confidence, courage, creativity, determination, energy, ego, friendship, leadership, loyalty, muse, passion, play, pleasure, power, pride, royalty, strength, warmth, willpower

Shadow side
Pride, has a tendency to brood

Things to do
Socialize with friends and family, get playful and enjoy life, be dramatic (in a productive and friendly way!), show off a little, get creative and paint, color, or draw, make love, finish a big project, go to the spa, go out dancing

Mantras
I am manifesting my creative dreams.
I love the life I have created.
I am the star of the show.

MOON IN VIRGO

Virgo Correspondences
House: 6th house

Element: Earth sign

Quality: Mutable sign

Season: Summer

Planet: Mercury

Colors: Navy blue, gold, dark grey, green, purple, yellow

Chakras: Sacral, solar plexus, throat

Body Parts: Digestive system, nervous system

Tarot: The Hermit

Herbs: Aster, bergamot, dill, hyacinth, lavender, lily, marjoram, rosemary, violet

Gemstones: Amazonite, aventurine, emerald, jade, lapis lazuli, lodestone, picture jasper, sapphire, sugilite, turquoise

Animals: Bee, cat, squirrel, sparrow

Keywords
Analytical, compulsive, critical, cycles, destiny, details, focus on work, grounded, herbalism, holistic, judgment, logic, mind, order, organization, practical, purification, success, thoughts, well-being, workaholic, worry

Shadow side
Can seem cold, demand perfection (of self and others)

Things to do
Take inventory, organize your space, clean up, clean out, donate things that are no longer needed. This is a good time to carry out previously made decisions, as well as start a new workout routine or heath regimine

Mantras
Perfection does not exist.
I am grounded by my routine.
I value myself for more than my work.

MOON IN LIBRA

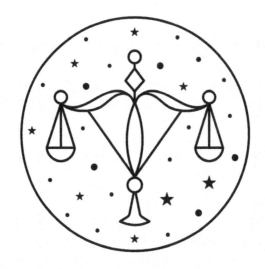

Libra Correspondences
House: 7th house

Element: Air sign

Quality: Cardinal sign

Season: Autumn

Planet: Venus

Colors: Light blue, black, yellow, green, pink, royal blue

Chakras: Sacral, heart

Body Parts: Kidneys, skin, lumbar region

Tarot: Empress

Herbs: Catnip, dandelion, foxglove, hazel, mugwort, passionflower, pennyroyal, rose, strawberry

Gemstones: Agate, ametrine, bloodstone, desert rose, kyanite, lepidolite, malachite, smoky quartz

Animals: Dove, hare, goose, raven, snake

Keywords
Balance, beauty, business, codependency, community, cooperation, counseling, feeling-based decision making, harmony, helping the environment/animals, justice, listening, love, marriage, peacemaker, relationships

Shadow work
Can overthink everything, delay decision making

Things to do
Have deep discussions with friends and family, do work that helps aid the environment or animals, attend social gatherings, tend to the balance of your world in all areas (inner/outer, spiritual/practical, work/life, mental/physical and so on), speak out for justice, fill your home with beauty, sign contracts

Mantras
I bring balance to my environment.
I am making the best decisions for myself.
I see the beauty all around me.

MOON IN SCORPIO

Scorpio Correspondences
House: 8th house

Element: Water sign

Quality: Fixed sign

Season: Autumn

Planets: Mars, Pluto

Colors: Black, blue, crimson, grey, red

Chakras: Root, sacral

Body Parts: Reproductive system, sexual organs

Tarot: Death

Herbs: Anemone, blackthorn, dill, gardenia, heather, ivy, pomegranate, saffron, valerian

Gemstones: Alexandrite, beryl, bloodstone, carnelian, citrine, garnet, red jasper, kunzite, labradorite, malachite, moonstone, snowflake obsidian, snakeskin agate, topaz, ruby, zircon

Animals: Dog, panther, wolf, eagle, phoenix, scorpion

Keywords
Authenticity, change, clairvoyance, control, creativity, darkness, death, deep feelings, desire, destruction, determination, emotions, introspection, intense, jealousy, love, lust, the otherworld, passion, power, psychic, rebirth, revenge, secrets, sexuality, spirituality, success, transformation, trust

Shadow side
Manipulation, negativity

Things to do
Get to the root of a problem, make a plan to get out of debt or increase savings, let go of things, see things from a higher perspective, make investments, have sex, consult a tarot deck, journal and pay attention to any intuitive nudges

Mantras
I am getting to the root of things.
My power is in the darkness.
I rise again.

MOON IN SAGITTARIUS

Sagittarius Correspondences
House: 9th house

Element: Fire sign

Quality: Mutable sign

Season: Autumn

Planet: Jupiter

Colors: Black, dark blue, gold, orange, purple, yellow

Chakras: Root, solar plexus, throat

Body Parts: Hips, thighs, liver

Tarot: Temperance

Herbs: Anise, aster, beech, carnation, chestnut, elder, mugwort, red clover, rowan, rose, spruce, vervain

Gemstones: Amethyst, azurite, herkimer diamond, iolite, labradorite, lapis lazuli, obsidian, peridot, star sapphire, sodalite, spinel, sugilite

Animals: Doe, elk, horse, lion, monkey

Keywords
Adventure, beauty, danger, dream work, drifting, energy, fear, freedom, free spirit, growth, higher perspective, honesty, independence, intuition, laid back, leadership, life goals, loyal, optimism, philosophy, travel, wanderer

Shadow side
Restless, blunt with words

Things to do
Plan for a trip, take a trip, travel, get away, study something new, take a class, plan or write down life goals, start a new spiritual practice, find a mentor, go to the library

Mantras
I am bringing my dreams to reality.
I brave the adventure of life.
I take aim at my goals.

MOON IN CAPRICORN

Capricorn Correspondences
House: 10th house

Element: Earth sign

Quality: Cardinal sign

Season: Winter

Planet: Saturn

Colors: Black, navy blue, brown, dark green, indigo, white

Chakras: Root, crown

Body Parts: Joints, skeletal system

Tarot: The Devil

Herbs: Aspen, carnation, comfrey, elder, jasmine, magnolia, poppy, rowan, sweet woodruff

Gemstones: Azurite, black agate, fluorite, garnet, hematite, jet, obsidian, onyx, pyrite, ruby, tiger's eye, turquoise

Animals: Dog, dolphin, elephant, falcon, goat, heron, owl

Keywords
Accomplishment, ambition, confidence, darkness, determination, father, focus, grounding, hard work, manifestation, masculinity, obstacles, patience, prosperity, responsibility, skills, strength, willpower

Shadow side
Pessimism, rigidity

Things to do
Sign paperwork, plan and commit to long term goals, pause and reflect on the past, see how far you've come, make a to-do list and plan ahead, be open to new beginnings, go for a hike

Mantras
I am reaching the top of my mountain.
I am strong and tender.
I am determined.

MOON IN AQUARIUS

Aquarius Correspondences
House: 11th house

Element: Air sign

Quality: Fixed sign

Season: Winter

Planets: Uranus, Saturn

Colors: Blue, green, indigo, turquoise, light yellow

Chakras: Throat, third eye, crown

Body Parts Circulatory system

Tarot: The Star

Herbs: Apple, ash, dandelion, foxglove, hawthorn, iris, lavender, mimosa, peppermint, pine, rosemary, sage

Gemstones: Amber, amethyst, aquamarine, amazonite, fluorite, garnet, hematite, jade, lepidolite, moss agate, opal

Animals: Dog, otter, sheep

Keywords
Commitments, debates, detachment, figuring things out, fixing things, group efforts, information, inspiration, logic, making improvements, upgrades

Shadow side
Self-absorption, can seem detached and cold

Things to do
Go with the flow, make improvements for the greater good, work with a team, be innovative, fix what's broken or needs to be upgraded, buy a new piece of technology, volunteer, invent something, go to a networking event, brainstorm solutions for a problem (perhaps even as a group!)

Mantras
I innovate for a better world.
I celebrate my difference.
Together we evolve.

MOON IN PISCES

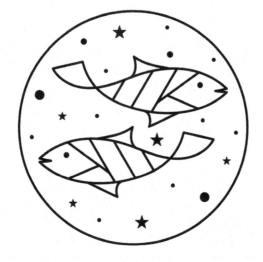

Pisces Correspondences
House: 12th house

Element: Water sign

Quality: Mutable sign

Season: Winter

Planets: Jupiter, Neptune

Colors: Light blue, light green, lavender, light yellow

Chakras: Third eye, crown

Body Parts: Feet, toes, lymphatic system

Tarot: The Moon

Herbs: Anise, catnip, gardenia, heliotrope, honeysuckle, jasmine, lavender, lily, sage, star anise

Gemstones: Alexandrite, amethyst, aquamarine, blue lace agate, diamond, fluorite, moonstone, ocean jasper, sugilite, black tourmaline, turquoise

Animals: Ox, horse, sheep

Keywords
Creativity, dream work, illusion, manifestation, metaphysical, not seeing clearly, spiritual in material

Shadow side
Over feel emotions, only focus on the negative

Things to do
Create something, connect with guides, work with your intuition (things like oracle decks can be good for this), play with your imagination, let yourself dream

Mantras
I bring my creative dreams to reality.
I celebrate my feelings.
I see the spiritual in the mundane.

NEW MOON
INTENTION

New Moon Date: _____
Time: _____
Sign: _____

How you feel: _____

_____
_____
_____

Intention: _____

_____
_____
_____
_____
_____

New Moon Journaling Space: _____

_____

_____

_____

_____

_____

_____

_____

_____

_____

_____

_____

_____

_____

_____

Action steps for the First Quarter Moon?

_____

_____

_____

_____

_____

_____

_____

How you feel at the Full Moon two weeks later:

_____

_____

_____

_____

_____

_____

_____

What you are releasing at the Last Quarter Moon:

_____

_____

_____

_____

_____

_____

_____

Follow up at the Full Moon six months after
the New Moon:

_____

_____

_____

_____

_____

_____

NEW MOON
INTENTION

New Moon Date: _____

Time: _____

Sign: _____

How you feel: _____

_____

_____

_____

Intention: _____

_____

_____

_____

_____

_____

New Moon Journaling Space: _____

_____

_____

_____

_____

_____

_____

_____

_____

_____

_____

_____

_____

_____

_____

_____

Action steps for the First Quarter Moon?

_____

_____

_____

_____

_____

_____

_____

_____

How you feel at the Full Moon two weeks later:

_____

_____

_____

_____

_____

_____

_____

_____

What you are releasing at the Last Quarter Moon:

_____

_____

_____

_____

_____

_____

_____

Follow up at the Full Moon six months after
the New Moon:

_____

_____

_____

_____

_____

NEW MOON
INTENTION

New Moon Date: _____
Time: _____
Sign: _____

How you feel: _____

_____

_____

_____

Intention: _____

_____

_____

_____

_____

_____

_____

New Moon Journaling Space: _____

_____

_____

_____

_____

_____

_____

_____

_____

_____

_____

_____

_____

_____

_____

_____

_____

Action steps for the First Quarter Moon?

_____

_____

_____

_____

_____

_____

_____

How you feel at the Full Moon two weeks later:

_____

_____

_____

_____

_____

_____

_____

What you are releasing at the Last Quarter Moon:

_____

_____

_____

_____

_____

_____

_____

_____

Follow up at the Full Moon six months after
the New Moon:

_____

_____

_____

_____

_____

_____

NEW MOON INTENTION

New Moon Date: _____
Time: _____
Sign: _____

How you feel: _____

_____

_____

_____

Intention: _____

_____

_____

_____

_____

_____

_____

New Moon Journaling Space: _____

_____

_____

_____

_____

_____

_____

_____

_____

_____

_____

_____

_____

_____

_____

_____

_____

Action steps for the First Quarter Moon?

_____

_____

_____

_____

_____

_____

_____

_____

How you feel at the Full Moon two weeks later:

_____

_____

_____

_____

_____

_____

_____

_____

What you are releasing at the Last Quarter Moon:

_____

_____

_____

_____

_____

_____

_____

_____

Follow up at the Full Moon six months after
the New Moon:

_____

_____

_____

_____

_____

_____

NEW MOON
INTENTION

New Moon Date: _____
Time: _____
Sign: _____

How you feel: _____

_____

_____

_____

Intention: _____

_____

_____

_____

_____

_____

New Moon Journaling Space: _____

_____

_____

_____

_____

_____

_____

_____

_____

_____

_____

_____

_____

_____

_____

_____

_____

Action steps for the First Quarter Moon?

_____

_____

_____

_____

_____

_____

_____

_____

How you feel at the Full Moon two weeks later:

_____

_____

_____

_____

_____

_____

_____

_____

What you are releasing at the Last Quarter Moon:

_____

_____

_____

_____

_____

_____

_____

_____

Follow up at the Full Moon six months after
the New Moon:

_____

_____

_____

_____

_____

_____

NEW MOON
INTENTION

New Moon Date: _____
Time: _____
Sign: _____

How you feel: _____

_____

_____

_____

Intention: _____

_____

_____

_____

_____

_____

_____

New Moon Journaling Space: _____

_____
_____
_____
_____
_____
_____
_____
_____
_____
_____
_____
_____
_____
_____
_____
_____
_____

Action steps for the First Quarter Moon?

_____

_____

_____

_____

_____

_____

_____

How you feel at the Full Moon two weeks later:

_____

_____

_____

_____

_____

_____

_____

What you are releasing at the Last Quarter Moon:

_____

_____

_____

_____

_____

_____

_____

Follow up at the Full Moon six months after
the New Moon:

_____

_____

_____

_____

_____

NEW MOON
INTENTION

New Moon Date: _____
Time: _____
Sign: _____

How you feel: _____

_____

_____

_____

Intention: _____

_____

_____

_____

_____

_____

New Moon Journaling Space: _____

_____

_____

_____

_____

_____

_____

_____

_____

_____

_____

_____

_____

_____

_____

_____

_____

Action steps for the First Quarter Moon?

_____

_____

_____

_____

_____

_____

_____

_____

How you feel at the Full Moon two weeks later:

_____

_____

_____

_____

_____

_____

_____

_____

What you are releasing at the Last Quarter Moon:

_____

_____

_____

_____

_____

_____

_____

Follow up at the Full Moon six months after
the New Moon:

_____

_____

_____

_____

_____

_____

NEW MOON
INTENTION

New Moon Date: _____
Time: _____
Sign: _____

How you feel: _____

_____

_____

_____

Intention: _____

_____

_____

_____

_____

_____

New Moon Journaling Space: _____

_____

_____

_____

_____

_____

_____

_____

_____

_____

_____

_____

_____

_____

_____

_____

Action steps for the First Quarter Moon?

_____

_____

_____

_____

_____

_____

_____

_____

How you feel at the Full Moon two weeks later:

_____

_____

_____

_____

_____

_____

_____

_____

What you are releasing at the Last Quarter Moon:

_____

_____

_____

_____

_____

_____

_____

_____

Follow up at the Full Moon six months after
the New Moon:

_____

_____

_____

_____

_____

_____

NEW MOON
INTENTION

New Moon Date: _____

Time: _____

Sign: _____

How you feel: _____

_____

_____

_____

Intention: _____

_____

_____

_____

_____

_____

_____

New Moon Journaling Space: _____

_____

_____

_____

_____

_____

_____

_____

_____

_____

_____

_____

_____

_____

_____

_____

_____

_____

Action steps for the First Quarter Moon?

_____

_____

_____

_____

_____

_____

_____

_____

How you feel at the Full Moon two weeks later:

_____

_____

_____

_____

_____

_____

_____

_____

What you are releasing at the Last Quarter Moon:

_____

_____

_____

_____

_____

_____

_____

Follow up at the Full Moon six months after
the New Moon:

_____

_____

_____

_____

_____

_____

NEW MOON
INTENTION

New Moon Date: _____
Time: _____
Sign: _____

How you feel: _____

_____

_____

_____

Intention: _____

_____

_____

_____

_____

_____

New Moon Journaling Space: _____

_____

_____

_____

_____

_____

_____

_____

_____

_____

_____

_____

_____

_____

_____

_____

_____

Action steps for the First Quarter Moon?

_____

_____

_____

_____

_____

_____

_____

_____

How you feel at the Full Moon two weeks later:

_____

_____

_____

_____

_____

_____

_____

_____

What you are releasing at the Last Quarter Moon:

_____

_____

_____

_____

_____

_____

_____

Follow up at the Full Moon six months after
the New Moon:

_____

_____

_____

_____

_____

_____

NEW MOON
INTENTION

New Moon Date: _____
Time: _____
Sign: _____

How you feel: _____

_____
_____
_____

Intention: _____

_____
_____
_____
_____
_____
_____

New Moon Journaling Space: _____

_____

_____

_____

_____

_____

_____

_____

_____

_____

_____

_____

_____

_____

_____

_____

Action steps for the First Quarter Moon?

_____

_____

_____

_____

_____

_____

_____

_____

How you feel at the Full Moon two weeks later:

_____

_____

_____

_____

_____

_____

_____

_____

What you are releasing at the Last Quarter Moon:

_____

_____

_____

_____

_____

_____

Follow up at the Full Moon six months after
the New Moon:

_____

_____

_____

_____

_____

NEW MOON
INTENTION

New Moon Date: _____
Time: _____
Sign: _____

How you feel: _____

_____

_____

_____

Intention: _____

_____

_____

_____

_____

_____

New Moon Journaling Space: _____

_____

_____

_____

_____

_____

_____

_____

_____

_____

_____

_____

_____

_____

_____

Action steps for the First Quarter Moon?

_____

_____

_____

_____

_____

_____

_____

How you feel at the Full Moon two weeks later:

_____

_____

_____

_____

_____

_____

_____

What you are releasing at the Last Quarter Moon:

_____

_____

_____

_____

_____

_____

_____

_____

Follow up at the Full Moon six months after
the New Moon:

_____

_____

_____

_____

_____

_____

YEAR IN REVIEW

Take note of the past year. What intentions came to fruition?
Over the year did you find that some methods of intention
setting worked better for you than others? Make any notes
that you need in this space.

_____

_____

_____

_____

_____

_____

_____

NEW MOONS
2020 - 2022

October 16, 2020	Libra New Moon
November 15, 2020	Scorpio New Moon
December 14, 2020	Sagittarius New Moon(eclipse)
January 13, 2021	Capricorn New Moon
February 11, 2021	Aquarius New Moon
March 13, 2021	Pisces New Moon
April 4, 2021	Aries New Moon
May 11, 2021	Taurus New Moon
June 10, 2021	Gemini New Moon (eclipse)
July 10, 2018	Cancer New Moon
August 8, 2021	Leo New Moon
September 7, 2021	Virgo New Moon
October 6, 2010	Libra New Moon
November 4, 2021	Scorpio New Moon
December 4, 2021	Sagittarius New Moon(eclipse)
January 2, 2022	Capricorn New Moon
February 1, 2022	Aquarius New Moon

March 2, 2022	Pisces New Moon
April 1, 2022	Aries New Moon
April 30, 2022	Taurus New Moon (eclipse)
May 30, 2022	Gemini New Moon
June 29, 2022	Cancer New Moon
July 29, 2022	Leo New Moon
August 27, 2022	Virgo New Moon
September 25, 2022	Libra New Moon
October 25, 2022	Scorpio New Moon (eclipse)
November 23, 2022	Sagittarius New Moon
December 23, 2022	Capricorn New Moon

ABOUT THE AUTHOR

Sara McCormick is an astrologer
and writer based in North Carolina.
When she's not dreaming, writing,
or gazing at the moon, Sara can
be found working in her garden,
playing with her son and trying
to convince her husband that they
have room for just one more cat.

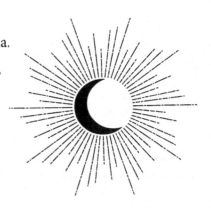

Follow her on Social Media
Twitter @bella_deluna
Facebook @belladelunaastrology
Instagram @belladelunaastrology

You can find more of her work on her website.

www.belladeluna.com